SEEING THE CIRCLE

by

Joseph Bruchac

photographs by

John Christopher Fine

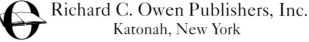

Richard C. Owen Publishers, Inc.
Katonah, New York

Richard C. Owen Publishers, Inc.
PO Box 585
Katonah, New York 10536

Library of Congress Cataloging-in-Publication Data

Bruchac, Joseph, 1942 -
        Seeing the circle / by Joseph Bruchac ; photographs by Joseph
Bruchac ; photographs by John Christopher Fine.
        p. cm. – (Meet the author)
    SUMMARY: The author tells how he learned about his own Native
American background, how he became a writer, and how he spends his
days.
    ISBN 1-57274-327-1
1. Bruchac, Joseph, 1942 - Juvenile literature. 2. Authors,
American – 20th century Biography Juvenile literature. 3. Indian
authors – United States Biography Juvenile literature. 4. Children's
stories – Authorship Juvenile literature. 5. Abenaki Indians
Biography Juvenile literature. [1. Bruchac, Joseph, 1942 -
2. Authors, American. 3. Abenaki Indians Biography. 4. Indians of
North America – New York (State) Biography.] I. Fine, John
Christopher, ill. II. Title . III. Series: Meet the author (Katonah, N.Y.)
    PS3552.R794 Z477 1999
    818' .5409–dc21
    [B]
                                          99-25330
                                            CIP

Editorial, Art, and Production Director   Janice Boland
Production Assistant   Donna Parsons

Color separations by Leo P. Callahan Inc., Binghamton, NY

Printed in the United States of America

9   8   7   6   5   4   3

To Barbara Kouts, literary agent and friend

How does the circle of my day begin?
I wake up early and look out the window at the mountains
east of our camp in Porter Corners, New York.
It's our second home, seven miles north of the old house
where I was raised.

Sometimes, I go straight to my study
because I woke up with an idea.
I need to write it down before I forget it.
It might be the start of a new story or a poem
or part of something I've already been working on.

I then spend half an hour doing exercises to African music.
Then it's time for breakfast – a fruit drink I make in the blender
with blueberries, watermelon, peaches, and cranberry juice.

After breakfast, my wife Carol and I walk with our dog Toni.
We hike around our pond or to the waterfall.

Carol is always the first one to read whatever I write.
I value her opinion. It's very important for writers
to have someone in their lives who will give them honest,
helpful feedback, the way a good teacher does for a student.
So, sometimes on our walks Carol and I talk about what I've written.
But I never discuss my ideas with anyone before I write them.

After our walk, I go into my study to write until noon.
Some days I know exactly what I want to say.
My words come out so fast I feel as if I'm taking dictation.

Other days I'm less certain, but I still try to write,
even if it is only a few words.
To be a writer, you have to write and keep writing.
Even if what you write isn't very good,
you can always revise it later and leave out
the parts that don't work.
But if you write nothing,
nothing is what you get!

After noon, it's down to the old house.
I read my mail – lots of it! I answer letters
from editors, other writers, friends, people who've invited me
to perform as a storyteller or to visit a school,
and from children who've read my books.

I may have to proofread the typeset manuscripts of my new books,
or I may talk on the phone with my literary agent,
who's also one of our best friends.

Sometimes I work with our older son, Jim.
Jim sells books by Indian writers.
He also teaches native outdoor awareness.
Our younger son Jesse tells traditional stories in Abenaki.

My mother put one hundred acres of our land
into a conservation easement so that it would stay forever wild.
Children and adults come from all over to learn
Native American skills and attend storytelling programs
in our longhouse. You'd be welcome, too.
Or you could visit our web sites at
ndakinna.com and nativeauthors.com.

The circle of my day changes with the seasons.
In late spring and summer I spend hours outside.
I prune the blueberries and raspberries at our camp.
I cut wood for our wood-burning stoves.
I work in the garden behind our old house.
It's the same garden my grandfather worked for fifty years.
As I do this work, I don't think about writing.

But later, when I sit down to write, ideas come to me
from the things I've done that day working outside.

Some days, especially in autumn and winter,
I pack a bag and Carol drives me to the airport in Albany.
I fly to distant cities and other states visiting schools,
performing at storytelling festivals,
and speaking at conferences about being a writer.

How did I become a storyteller and a writer
of children's books?

Young people often ask me that when I visit their schools. They're surprised when I tell them that I never planned to be a storyteller or writer. All through school, I wanted to be a naturalist.

They also ask what it was like growing up as a real Native American. They are even more surprised when I tell them that we never talked about our Indian heritage when I was a child.

When I was very young, I lived with my mother's parents,
and they would never mention our Indian blood.
Why? Back then it was shameful or even dangerous
to be identified as Indian.

My Abenaki grandfather was
dark skinned and looked Indian.
But whenever anyone asked him if he
was Indian, he had one simple answer.
"I'm French," he would say.
Being Indian was our family secret.
If you could pass for white,
your life would be safer and better.

My two younger sisters lived a quarter mile away
with my parents.   My father's parents came from Czechoslovakia.
We never talked about the European part of my ancestry either.

How did I end up known around the world
as a Native American storyteller and writer?
It all started with listening.
In my early twenties, Harold Tantaquidgeon, a Mohegan elder,
showed me the design of a circle divided into four sections.

The design stands for your four ancestors – two grandmothers and two grandfathers. It also stands for the four directions: East, South, West, and North.

The first part of the Circle represents the dawn
and the first step to learning, which is to listen.
The second part of the Circle stands for the morning
and the second step, which is to observe.
The third part of the Circle is the afternoon
and it reminds us to remember.
The fourth part of the Circle represents the sunset
and the final step to learning, which is to share.
"Listen," said Harold Tantaquidgeon.
"Listen."

I understood listening. My grandparents ran a store
in the Adirondack mountain foothills.
They called it Bowman's Store.
People sat around the old wood stove and told stories.
I hid behind the soda cabinet and listened.
I listened long after my bedtime.
There was no television to watch then.
Instead I listened to stories.

Being a listener led me to reading.
Grampa Jesse could barely read or write.
He quit school in the fourth grade when he jumped out the window
because other kids kept calling him a dirty Indian.
But Grampa was proud that I was a good reader
and had me read aloud to him.

My grandmother was a graduate of Albany Law School.
Because of her, our house was full of books.
There were novels, history books, poetry,
and books about far-away lands, especially Africa and its wildlife!
Someday, I promised myself, I'd go to Africa.
Whenever I wanted a new book to read
Grama drove me to the Saratoga Springs Library.
The downstairs children's room was one of my two favorite places
in the world. There I found *Babar*, *Charlotte's Web*,
and *Mr. Popper's Penguins*.

My second-favorite place was the woods behind our house.
There my grandfather pointed out things to me
like squirrels' nests and animal tracks and bloodroots,
the first flowers after snow.
When I grew up and became a father,
I pointed those things out to my own sons.

Being a reader led me to writing.

I loved poems and started memorizing poetry as soon as I could talk.

I began writing poems in the second grade, and I've never stopped.

What was I like when I was young?

Well, I was the kind of kid none of the other kids liked.

I was a little know-it-all with glasses. I was scared of being beaten up, and I was also a tattletale.

If you'd known me when I was a kid,

I think you wouldn't have liked me.

Adults sometimes imagine childhood is easy.

I'd never want to be a child again.

It's just plain awful to be a kid who's different.

But the great thing about life is that you can grow and change.

In high school I changed from a bookworm
to a football player and champion wrestler.
I was still the same person inside,
but people who had picked on me now wanted to be my friends.
After high school I went to Cornell University
to study wildlife conservation. I still planned to be a naturalist.
There I became a varsity heavyweight wrestler.

People who hadn't met me before thought I was just a dumb athlete.
They didn't know I was a reader, a poet, and a writer.
Again I was judged by how I looked.
Now, though, it made me laugh.

23

Two of the three best things in my adult life
happened to me at Cornell.
The first was when a friend of mine introduced
me to his sister Carol. A little over a year later
Carol and I were married.

The second best thing was a course in creative writing
taught by a poet named Robert Sward.
I did so well that I switched my major to English.
I kept wrestling, but now I also edited
the school literary magazine.

After Cornell, guess where I went? Africa!
Carol and I volunteered for a program called Teachers for West Africa.
For three years I taught English at a school in Ghana.

AFRICA

Ghana

The third best thing was fatherhood.

In 1968 our first son, James, was born.

Our second son, Jesse, was born in 1972.

I wanted my children to learn about their Indian heritage.

How would I teach them?

I would tell them stories.

I traveled the country seeking Native elders.

I listened. I read books. I researched.

And I learned.

Being a father made me a storyteller.

After Ghana, we came home to Grampa Jesse.
We had circled back to Bowman's Store and my childhood home.
We also spent lots of time with my mother and father.
I'd lived my childhood apart from them, but now we wanted our
children to know their grandparents. As I listened to my father's
stories the distance between us closed. I taught at Skidmore College
and wrote. My poems were published in hundreds of magazines. My
first book of poetry was called *Indian Mountain*.

When the editors of a poetry magazine decided to publish
children's books, they asked me to send them a manuscript
of stories I told my own children. We called the book *Turkey Brother
and Other Iroquois Stories*. It was illustrated by my Mohawk friend
John Kahionhes Fadden. Kahionhes also illustrated *Keepers of the
Earth*, a series of books I co-authored with Michael Caduto.
Keepers of the Earth uses traditional Native American stories
to teach natural science.

In 1981, I resigned from Skidmore College.

I became a full-time storyteller and writer.

My first picture book was *Thirteen Moons on Turtle's Back*.

It was Jonathan London's idea.

He wanted to write a book about the Moons

as Native people name them.

He asked me for advice.

We wrote letter after letter to each other.

Finally, he asked me to be co-author!

That book introduced me to one of my favorite illustrators,

Thomas Locker.

I'm always writing at least two or three books at the same time.
As soon as I finish one, I start another.

SACAGAWEA'S JOURNEY
by Joseph Bruchac

ST. LOUIS, 1811

CHAPTER ONE:
THE CAMP BY THE RIVER

We were poor people. That is how it was then, my son. We were not as poor as our cousins who lived further downriver and toward the direction of the sunset. They were so poor that they had no horses at all. All of the other tribes called them Walkers. At least we had horses.

We were poor because we had no guns as did the Atsina and Siksika. As did the other nations who lived close to the French and English and American traders. Those other nations had driven us off the plains and up into the mountains with their guns.

But, poor as we were, we still had horses. We cared for our horses well. Our horses were like members of our families. Even though we were often hungry, we would never eat our horses. Not like the white men did. But that was later, much later.

With horses our young men could go back down the mountains and slip out onto the plains to hunt the buffalo. They had to always be on the lookout for enemies, but our horses were swift and the scouts were alert. On the plains you can see enemies coming from far away and

I read constantly, both for research
and for fun. I read at least one book a day,
as well as newspapers and magazines.
I photocopy and save articles that interest me.
Sometimes an article in a newspaper
will start me off on a whole new book.

I also keep journals where I write down ideas,
conversations, or parts of poems.
Sometimes something I wrote in my journal
long ago will turn into a poem or story.

Do I revise my work? You bet!
If you want to be a writer, you have to do lots of revising.
I'm a good writer, but a great re-writer!
I've also been blessed with understanding editors.
In many ways, my editors are like your teachers.
They read what I write and suggest how to make it better.

Our sons grew up to be professional storytellers and writers.
And so the Circle goes on. Let me pass the Circle to you.
Remember to listen.

Listen to your teachers.
Listen to your elders.
Listen to each other.
Listen to all the stories around you.
Most of all, listen to your heart.

Peace,

Other Books by Joseph Bruchac

A Boy Called Slow; The Arrow Over the Door; Between Earth and Sky; Eagle Song; Fox Song; Keepers of the Night; Near the Mountains; The Girl Who Married the Moon; The Heart of a Chief; The First Strawberries; Thirteen Moons on Turtle's Back; When the Chenoo Howls

About the Photographer

John Christopher Fine, a marine biologist, is the author of award-winning books about ocean pollution. John travels to exciting and interesting places throughout the world taking photographs. He spent several days with Joseph and his family taking the pictures for this book.

Acknowledgments

Photographs on pages 11, 16, 17, 20, 22, 23, 24, 25, and 26 appear courtesy of Joseph Bruchac. Painting on page 18 of Harold Tantaquidgeon appears courtesy of the Mohegan Nation. Book covers on page 27 from *Keepers of Life: Discovering Plants Through Native American Stories and Earth Activities for Children*, copyright 1994 by Michael J. Caduto and Joseph Bruchac, cover design by Chris Bierwirth, cover illustration by John Kahionhes Fadden, permission granted by Fulcrum Publishing; *Keepers of the Earth: Native American Stories and Environmental Activities for Children*, copyright 1988, 1989 by Michael J. Caduto and Joseph Bruchac, cover design by Chris Bierwirth, cover illustration by John Kahionhes Fadden, permission granted by Fulcrum Publishing; and *Keepers of the Animals; Native American Stories and Wildlife Activities for Children*, copyright 1991 by Michael J. Caduto and Joseph Bruchac, cover design by Chris Bierwirth, cover illustration by John Kahionhes Fadden, permission granted by Fulcrum Publishing. Illustration on page 28 from *Water Dance*, copyright 1992 by Joseph Bruchac and Jonathan London, illustrations copyright 1992 by Thomas Locker, used by permission of Philomel, a division of Penguin Putnam, Inc. Cover illustration on page 30 from *Flying with the Eagle, Racing the Great Bear: Stories from Native North America*, copyright 1993 by Joseph Bruchac. Illustrations copyright 1993 by Murv Jacob. Used by permission of BridgeWater Books, an imprint of Troll Associates. Cover illustration on page 30 from *The Arrow Over the Door*, copyright 1998 by Joseph Bruchac. Illustrations copyright 1998 by James Watling. Used by permission of Dial Books for Young Readers, a member of Penguin Putnam, Inc.